What's in this book

This book belongs to

_____

生病了 I'm sick!

学习内容 Contents

沟通 Communication

说说身体健康情况
Talk about physical health

生词 New words

★	生病	to be sick
★	看病	to see a doctor
★	生气	angry
★	医生	doctor
★	护士	nurse
★	药	medicine
★	等	to wait
★	应该	should
	讨厌	to hate
	健康	healthy
	打针	to have an injection

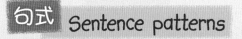 **Sentence patterns**

我应该去看病。
I should see a doctor.

我们不应该淘气。
We should not be so naughty.

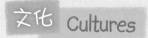 **Cultures**

传统中医
Traditional Chinese medicine

 **Project**

认识健康生活方式
Learn about the healthy lifestyle

Get ready

1 Are you healthy?

2 Do you like going to the doctor's when you are sick?

3 Do you think Ivan is dressed warm enough? What might happen?

艾文感冒了，妈妈要带他去看病，
但是他讨厌打针和吃药。

艾文不想去看病。伊森假装生病了，
穿着弟弟的衣服等妈妈。

hù shi

护士

"你是下一个，艾文。"护士叫病人的
名字。伊森很紧张。

健康

医生

"他很健康，没生病。"医生向妈妈说。伊森脸红了，低下头。

shēng qì
生气

"对不起，医生，我弟弟讨厌看病，我代替他来。"伊森说。妈妈很生气。

"我应该去看病的。"艾文说。"对不起，妈妈，我们不应该淘气。"伊森说。

Let's think

1 Recall the story. Put a tick or a cross.

2 Look at the pictures and discuss them with your friend. Have you had any check-ups before?

我的眼睛……
所以和他一样，
也要……

她的牙很疼，
所以……

她可能生
病了……

他的身体不舒服，
医生在……

New words

1 Learn the new words.

2 Listen to your teacher and point to the correct words above.

🎧 03 **1** Listen and number the pictures.

🎧 04 **2** Look at the pictures. Listen to the story a

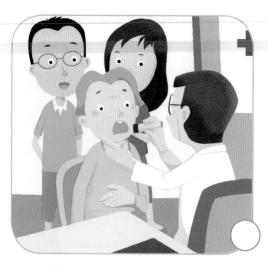

护士，请问我是下一个吗？

是的，你在这里等一等，很快到你了。

你的身体很好，非常健康。

太好啦！因为我天天运动。

医生，我不喜欢生病，因为我讨厌打针和吃药。

你还应该多吃蔬菜和水果，知道吗？

我知道了，谢谢医生！

3 Role-play with your friend.

1 女孩的头很疼，她可能生病了。

她应该……

2 我明天要数学考试了。

你应该……

3 他们找不到火车站了。

我们……帮助他们。

Task

Look at the picture and read the boy's letter. Talk to your friend about a time that he/she was sick.

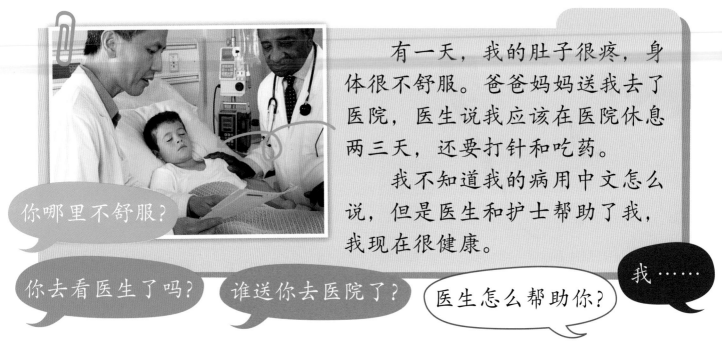

有一天，我的肚子很疼，身体很不舒服。爸爸妈妈送我去了医院，医生说我应该在医院休息两三天，还要打针和吃药。

我不知道我的病用中文怎么说，但是医生和护士帮助了我，我现在很健康。

你哪里不舒服？

你去看医生了吗？

谁送你去医院了？

医生怎么帮助你？

我……

Game

Play a doctor-patient game with your friends.

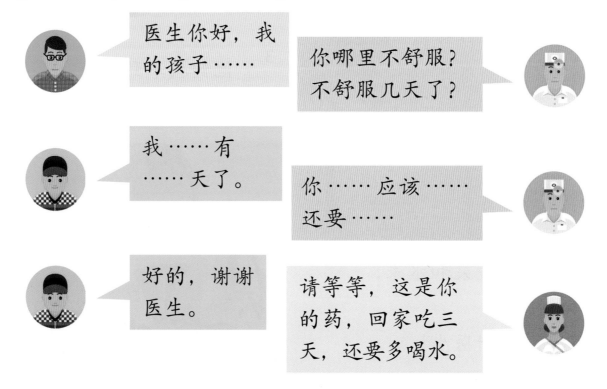

医生你好，我的孩子……

你哪里不舒服？不舒服几天了？

我……有……天了。

你……应该……还要……

好的，谢谢医生。

请等等，这是你的药，回家吃三天，还要多喝水。

Chant

 05 Listen and say.

小朋友呀小朋友，
生病应该怎么办？
医生护士帮助你，
打针吃药多喝水。
爸爸妈妈帮助你，
多吃蔬菜和水果。
天天早起做运动，
身体健康快乐多。

生活用语 Daily expressions

真讨厌！
So disgusting!

请等等。
Please wait.

1 Trace and write the characters.

一 丁 丆 匸 豕 矢 医

丿 𠂉 𠂢 牛 生

医	生	医	生
医	生		

丶 亠 广 广 应 应

丶 讠 讠 讠 讨 该 该

应	该	应	该
应	该		

医
生
应
该

2 Write and say.

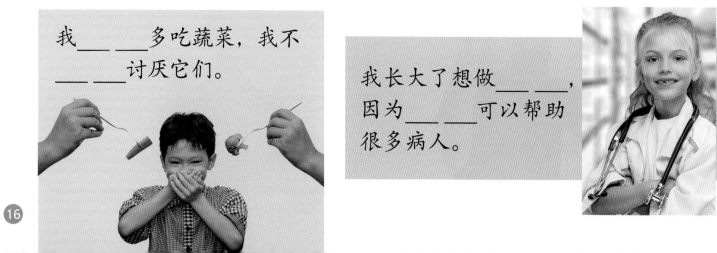

我 ___ ___ 多吃蔬菜，我不
___ ___ 讨厌它们。

我长大了想做 ___ ___，
因为 ___ ___ 可以帮助
很多病人。

3 Read, circle the wrong words and write the correct ones. There is one mistake in each line.

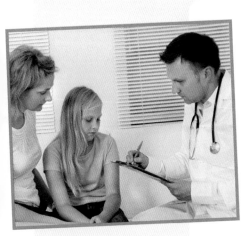

这几天，找觉得很累，也不   1   _____

相吃东西，更不想去上学。妈妈   2   _____

带我去看医王。医生说我生病了，   3   _____

应孩吃三天药。   4   _____

现在，我的病慢慢孩起来   5   _____

了，我也开心多了。

拼音输入法 Pinyin input

Match the dialogue by drawing lines. Then type the whole dialogue in the right order.

1 你哪儿不舒服？ •	• 好的，谢谢医生。
2 不舒服几天了？ •	• 我头疼，觉得很累，可能是感冒了。
3 你先吃两天的药，回家好好休息，多喝水，知道吗？ •	• 昨天上午还好好的，晚上开始头疼了。

Cultures

Have you heard of traditional Chinese medicine? Learn about it.

Traditional Chinese medicine (TCM, 中医) has been practised for more than 2,500 years and has many different forms.

TCM is widely used in China and is becoming more popular all over the world.

Herbal medicine mostly uses plants. Herbs are grouped according to their effects on the body.

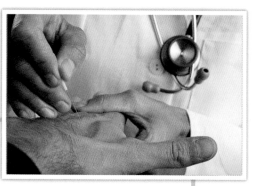

Acupuncture helps reduce pain and treats various medical conditions.

Qi gong is practised for exercise, preventive medicine and medical treatment.

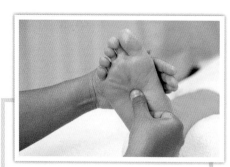

Tui na is a body treatment that gets the energy moving in the body.

Dietary therapy is based on the effects of food on the human body.

Project

1 Learn about healthy and unhealthy lifestyles. Which lifestyle is yours?

健康的生活
Healthy Lifestyle

不健康的生活
Unhealthy Lifestyle

2 Talk to your friend to see if you have a healthy lifestyle. Can you give good advice on healthy living?

我放学后和哥哥一起去踢足球，晚上只看一小时电视。

我不坐公共汽车上学，我现在天天骑自行车上学。

我再也不……
因为……

我觉得我们应该……

温习 Checkpoint

1 Complete the conversation and role-play with your friend.

2 Work with your friend. Colour the stars and the chillies.

Words	说	读	写
生病	☆	☆	🌶
看病	☆	☆	🌶
生气	☆	☆	🌶
医生	☆	☆	☆
护士	☆	☆	🌶
药	☆	☆	🌶
等	☆	☆	🌶
应该	☆	☆	☆

Words and sentences	说	读	写
讨厌	☆	🌶	🌶
健康	☆	🌶	🌶
打针	☆	🌶	🌶
我应该去看病。	☆	☆	🌶
我们不应该淘气。	☆	☆	🌶

Talk about physical health	☆

3 What does your teacher say?

My teacher says ...

分享 Sharing

Words I remember

生病	shēng bìng	to be sick
看病	kàn bìng	to see a doctor
生气	shēng qì	angry
医生	yī shēng	doctor
护士	hù shi	nurse
药	yào	medicine
等	děng	to wait
应该	yīng gāi	should
讨厌	tǎo yàn	to hate
健康	jiàn kāng	healthy
打针	dǎ zhēn	to have an injection

Other words

感冒	gǎn mào	to have a cold
带	dài	to take
假装	jiǎ zhuāng	to pretend
病人	bìng rén	patient
紧张	jǐn zhāng	nervous
低头	dī tóu	to lower one's head
代替	dài tì	to replace
淘气	táo qì	naughty
生活	shēng huó	life

OXFORD
UNIVERSITY PRESS

Oxford University Press is a department of the University of Oxford.
It furthers the University's objective of excellence in research, scholarship,
and education by publishing worldwide. Oxford is a registered trade mark of
Oxford University Press in the UK and in certain other countries

Published in Hong Kong by
Oxford University Press (China) Limited
39th Floor, One Kowloon, 1 Wang Yuen Street, Kowloon Bay,
Hong Kong

Illustrated by Ah Lun, Anne Lee, KY Chan and Wildman

Photographs for reproduction permitted by Dreamstime.com

China National Publications Import & Export (Group) Corporation is an authorized distributor of
Oxford Elementary Chinese.
Please contact content@cnpiec.com.cn or 86-10-65856782

ISBN: 978-0-19-082309-2

10 9 8 7 6 5 4 3 2